A Word About
Horses

By Lynne Gibbs   Illustrated by Kristine Nason

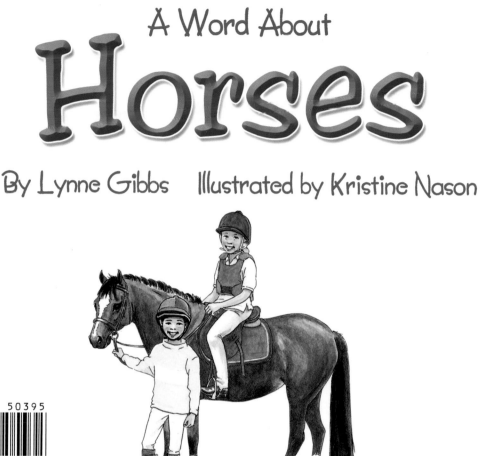

ISBN 0-7696-3387-0

50395

9 780769 633879

School Specialty Publishing

First published in Great Britain in 2005 by Brimax
Publishing Ltd, Appledram Barns, Chichester PO20 7EQ
Copyright © 2005 Brimax Publishing Ltd
This edition published in 2005 by Brighter Child®, an
imprint of School Specialty Publishing, a member of the
School Specialty Family. Printed in China.

Library of Congress Cataloging-in-Publication
Data is on file with the publisher.

Send all inquiries to:
School Specialty Publishing
8720 Orion Place
Columbus, OH 43240-2111

ISBN 0-7696-3387-0

2 3 4 5 6 7 0 9 10 BHI 10 09 08 07 06

Columbus, Ohio

The Points of a Horse

Each part of the horse has a different name, called a *point*. The points shown here are some of the most important parts of a horse.

Measuring a horse

Horses are measured in "hands." One hand is equal to about 4 inches. A horse's height is measured from the withers (shoulder) to the ground. A pony is a horse that measures under 13 hands.

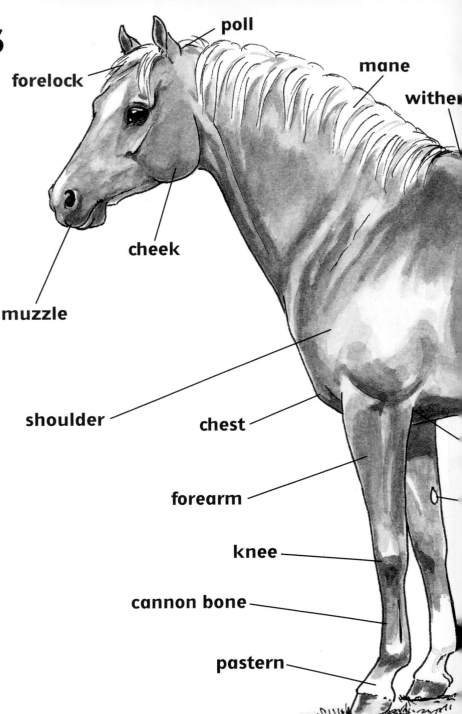

poll

mane

wither

forelock

cheek

muzzle

shoulder

chest

forearm

knee

cannon bone

pastern

2

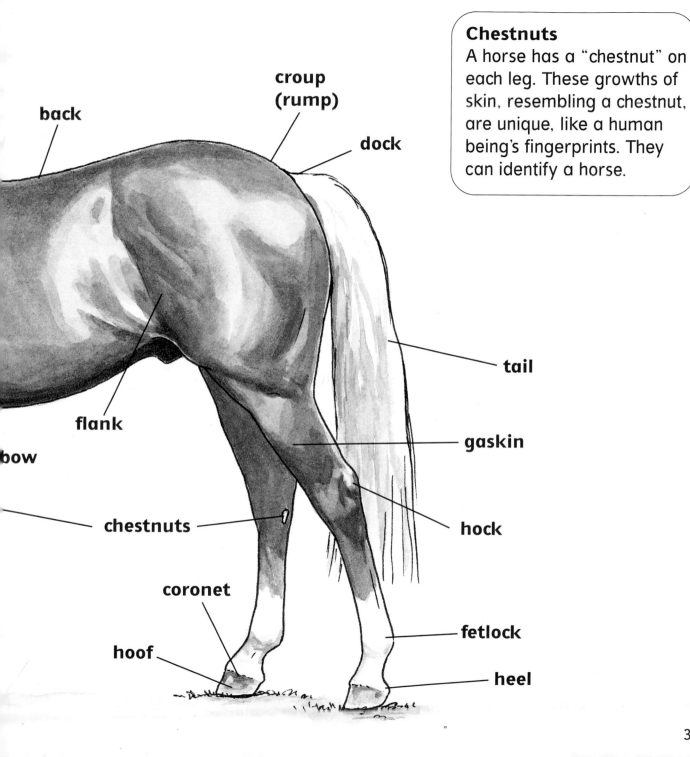

back

croup
(rump)

dock

Chestnuts
A horse has a "chestnut" on
each leg. These growths of
skin, resembling a chestnut,
are unique, like a human
being's fingerprints. They
can identify a horse.

tail

flank

bow

gaskin

chestnuts

hock

coronet

hoof

fetlock

heel

3

Jobs Around a Horse Stable

There are many jobs to do around a
horse stable. Horses need to be washed and groomed.
The stalls and fenced-in areas should be cleaned every day. It is
important to keep the stables, grounds, and horses in good condition.

5

Grooming

Here are some of the tools used for grooming. Stabled horses should be groomed every day. Grooming helps prevent disease. It also keeps a horse's coat clean and shiny.

hoof pick

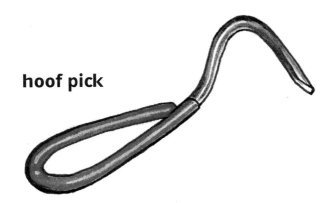

A hoof pick is used to clean dirt and stones from the horse's feet, working downwards from the heel towards the toe.

grooming brush

A grooming brush is used to remove dried mud, dirt, and dust from a horse's coat.

finishing brush

A finishing brush removes dust and dandruff from the coat, mane, and tail.

curry comb

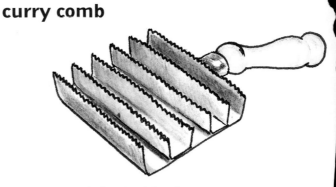

A curry comb is used to clean the finishing brush.

rubber curry comb

A rubber curry comb is another grooming tool used to remove dried mud from a horse's coat.

scrub brush

A damp scrub brush is used on the horse's mane, tail, and feet. It can also be used to remove stable stains.

finishing cloth

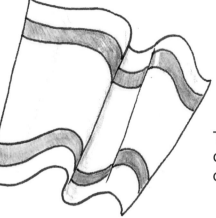

The finishing cloth adds a final polish after grooming.

sponges

Separate sponges are needed to clean a horse's eye and muzzle, and the dock area.

Horses in the pasture

A finishing brush should never be used over the whole body of a horse kept in the pasture. There should be some grease left in the coat to help keep rain out. A grooming brush or rubber curry comb should be used instead to remove dried mud and dirt.

Getting Ready to Ride

These children are preparing to ride their horses. They put on and adjust their saddles, bridles, and bits before they ride. Both the horse and the rider must be comfortable and safe.

Saddles and Stirrups

Different type of saddles are used for a variety of equestrian (horse riding) sports, including racing, show jumping, dressage, and polo.

all-purpose saddle

The all-purpose saddle can be used for most equestrian activities such as pleasure riding, hunting, and jumping.

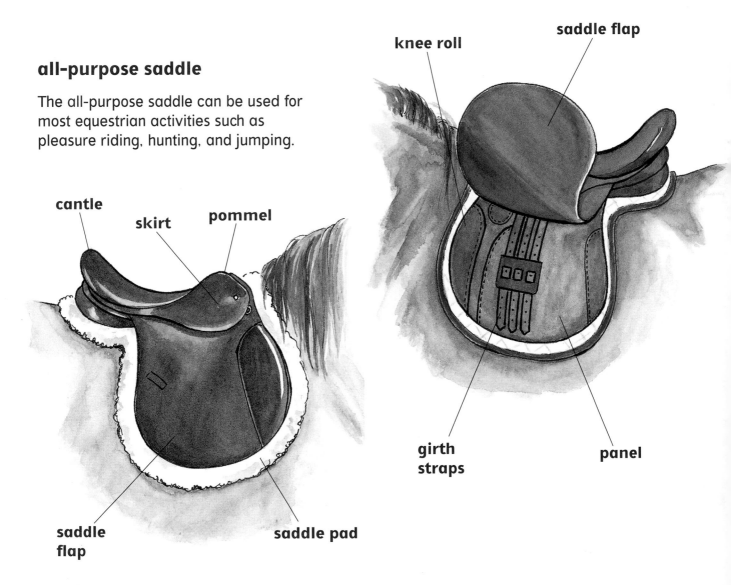

knee roll

saddle flap

cantle

skirt

pommel

girth straps

panel

saddle flap

saddle pad

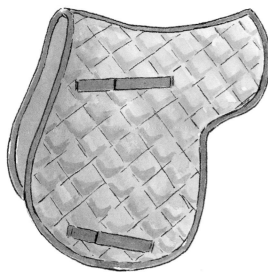

girth

Usually made of leather, nylon, or human-made fiber, a girth is placed under the horse's belly and holds the saddle in place.

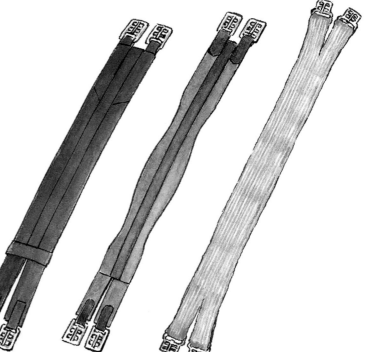

saddle pad

In addition to keeping the saddle clean, saddle pads are often used under the saddle to give extra comfort to the rider and the horse's back.

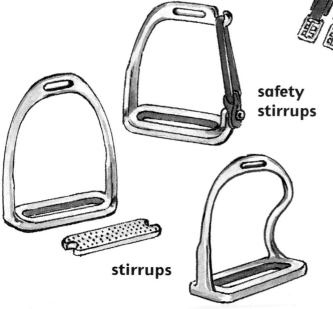

safety stirrups

stirrups

stirrups

Stirrups hang from the saddle and support a rider's feet. Stirrups should be made of stainless steel. Safety stirrups help prevent a rider's foot from becoming tangled in the stirrup should the rider fall from the horse.

Horse-Riding Equipment

These children are wearing the proper horse-riding equipment while they ride their horses.

Proper equipment is used for both comfort and safety. Helmets protect the head from falls and reflective vests notify drivers if the horse is ridden on the road.

These saddles and helmets are used for riding English style. The other style of riding is Western, where broad-brimmed hats are worn and the saddles are longer.

Bridles and Bits

A bridle supports the bit in the horse's mouth. The reins are attached to the bit and give the rider some control over the horse's speed.

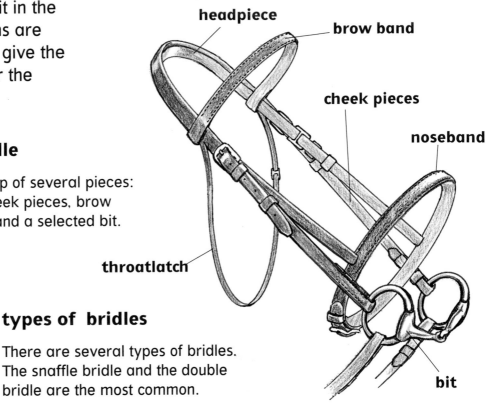

headpiece

brow band

cheek pieces

noseband

throatlatch

bit

parts of a bridle

A bridle is made up of several pieces: the headpiece, cheek pieces, brow band, noseband, and a selected bit.

types of bridles

There are several types of bridles. The snaffle bridle and the double bridle are the most common.

snaffle bridle

The snaffle bridle is the simplest and most widely used. It has a single rein and either a jointed or straight bit.

double bridle

The double bridle is used mainly for showing. It has two bits, each with separate reins.

nosebands

There are several types of nosebands. Which one to use depends on the habits of the horse.

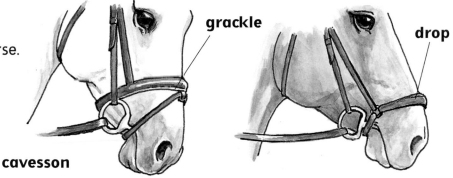

grackle

drop

cavesson

The standard noseband is the cavesson. The drop noseband is used on horses that tend to pull and need to close their lower jaws.

bits

The bit is attached to the bridle and rests on the horse's tongue. A bit is controlled by the reins and helps to position the horse's head and control its pace and direction.

kimblewick

pelham

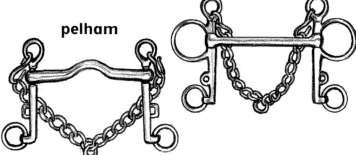

curb and bridoon

eggbutt snaffle

types of bits

Different bits are used depending on whether the horse is strong in the mouth or which equestrian discipline you are competing in. For example, a snaffle is used on horses with a soft mouth.

A Horse Stable

tack room

manger

PLEASE KEEP
GATE SHUT AT
ALL TIMES

This is an overview of a horse stable.
Equipment, food, and storage areas are identified by name.

bedding storage   **hay storage**   **water point**

gate

drainage

muck-heap

Stables and Fields

Stable areas vary in design according to their use and the number of horses being stabled. But there are some general rules that apply to all stables and fields.

trough

The water trough should always be filled with fresh, clean drinking water for the horses.

feed bucket

There is a variety of feed buckets, including fixed corner buckets, portable buckets that fit on the door, or buckets that sit on the ground.

manure

Stables should be cleaned out (mucked) every day, and the manure should be kept away from the area.

fields

The fields where horses roam and graze must be free of poisonous plants. Fields should be checked every day for broken fencing, rabbit or groundhog holes, and trash.

run-in shed

A run-in shed is an open-sided building in the field where horses go to rest. During the summer, it gives shelter from the heat, rain, and flies. In winter, it provides shelter from the cold and snow.

hay storage

Horses like to eat good quality hay. The amount of hay fed depends on the size of the horse and the amount of exercise it gets. Hay needs to be stored in a dry area so it does not become moldy.

tack room

All the equipment needed to ride a horse, such as saddles and bridles, are stored in a tack room.

stable

A horse's stable is its bedroom—a warm, snug place for the horse to sleep and relax. It should be kept clean and dry with fresh bedding.

Horse Jumping

After young riders have experience riding, they can begin jumping with their horses. When jumping, it is important to have the necessary horse-riding equipment and to have an adult nearby.

Jumping

Show jumping is one of the most popular equestrian sports.
Inexperienced riders start by learning to jump over very low obstacles.

trotting poles and cross poles

Riders first learn to trot and canter over poles
on the ground. They can then advance to
small cross poles.

uprights and spreads

Once they have mastered cross poles,
young riders can advance to upright
and spread fences.

As riders become more experienced,
the fences become more difficult.

triple bar

The triple bar is a spread fence
with three sets of poles built in a
stair-step pattern, with the highest
pole at the back.

parallel bars

The parallel bar is one of the most difficult
fences to jump. It can be made of poles or
planks.

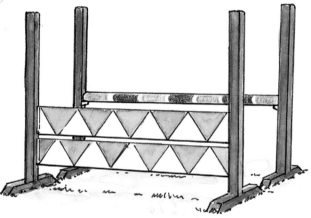

water jump

As its name implies, the water jump
in a show-jumping event has a sunken
trough of water. A smaller, narrower
water tray is used when a fence is
included in the obstacle.

Glossary

bedding Straw, wood shavings, or shredded paper used to line the floor of a horse's stable for warmth and to prevent the horse from injuring itself.

bit Attached to the bridle and rests on the horse's tongue. It controls the pace and direction of a horse.

bridle A leather strap that supports the bit in the horse's mouth.

canter A 3-beat gait that is slower than a gallop.

chestnut A growth of skin, resembling a chestnut, on each leg of the horse that is unique, like a human being's fingerprints.

dressage The art of training a horse to perform movements in a balanced, obedient manner.

girth Usually made of leather, this strap goes under the belly of the horse and keeps the saddle in place.

grooming Taking care of a horse by using special tools that keep its coat and hoofs in good condition.

hands The term used to measure horses. One hand is equal to four inches.

helmet Worn on the head to protect the rider.

jodhpurs Riding pants that fit closely from knee to ankle.

muck To clean out, as manure from a horse's stall.

noseband A strap that fits across a horse's nose. The type used depends on the habits of the horse.

paddock The compound where a horse is housed, exercised, and fed.

point Each part of the horse.

pony A horse that measures under 13 hands.

run-in shed An open-sided building where horses can go to rest or get out of the weather.

saddle pad Used under the saddle, it provides extra comfort for both the horse and the rider.

stable Like a bedroom, a warm, snug place for a horse to sleep and relax.

stirrups Hung from the saddle, they support the rider's feet.

tack The equipment worn by the horse, such as the saddle, the bridle, and the bit.

tack room A place where the horse's equipment is stored.

trot A moderately fast gait where the horse's legs run in diagonal pairs.